LAURIE HERNANDEZ

OLYMPIC GYMNAST

KATIE LAJINESS

Big Buddy Books

An Imprint of Abdo Publishing
abdopublishing.com

BIG BUDDY OLYMPIC BIOGRAPHIES

abdopublishing.com

Published by Abdo Publishing, a division of ABDO, PO Box 398166, Minneapolis, Minnesota 55439.
Copyright © 2017 by Abdo Consulting Group, Inc. International copyrights reserved in all countries.
No part of this book may be reproduced in any form without written permission from the publisher.
Big Buddy Books™ is a trademark and logo of Abdo Publishing.

Printed in the United States of America, North Mankato, Minnesota.
102016
012017

THIS BOOK CONTAINS
RECYCLED MATERIALS

Cover Photo: ASSOCIATED PRESS
Interior Photos: ASSOCIATED PRESS (pp. 6, 11, 13, 14, 19, 23); Evan Agostini/Invision/AP (p. 27);
    KGC-146/STAR MAX/IPx/AP (p. 29); Shutterstock (p. 9); Sipa USA via AP (pp. 21, 25);
    ZUMA Press, Inc./Alamy Stock Photo (pp. 5, 17, 23).

Coordinating Series Editor: Tamara L. Britton
Graphic Design: Jenny Christensen

Publisher's Cataloging-in-Publication Data

Names: Lajiness, Katie, author.
Title: Laurie Hernandez / by Katie Lajiness.
Description: Minneapolis, MN : Abdo Publishing, 2017. | Series: Big buddy
    Olympic biographies | Includes bibliographical references and index.
Identifiers: LCCN 2016953147 | ISBN 9781680785524 (lib. bdg.) |
    ISBN 9781680785807 (ebook)
Subjects: LCSH: Hernandez, Laurie, 2000- --Juvenile literature. | Women
    gymnasts--United States--Biography--Juvenile literature. | Women Olympic
    athletes--United States--Biography--Juvenile literature. | Olympic Games
    (31st : 2016 : Rio de Janeiro, Brazil)
Classification: DDC 794.44/092 [B]--dc23
LC record available at http://lccn.loc.gov/2016953147

CONTENTS

OLYMPIC STAR 4

SNAPSHOT 5

FAMILY TIES 6

EARLY YEARS 8

STARTING OUT 10

ELITE GYMNAST 14

ALL-AROUND SUPERSTAR 16

THE FINAL FIVE 18

OLYMPIC PERFORMANCE 22

FAN FAVORITE 24

OUTSIDE THE GYM 26

BUZZ 28

GLOSSARY 30

WEBSITES 31

INDEX 32

OLYMPIC STAR

Laurie Hernandez is a famous gymnast. She has won **competitions** all around the world. Laurie is only the fourth Hispanic **athlete** to ever make the Olympic women's gymnastics team.

In 2016, Laurie won two **medals** at the Olympics. She took home one gold for the team all-around event. And, she won a silver medal for the balance beam.

SNAPSHOT

NAME:
Lauren "Laurie"
Hernandez

BIRTHDAY:
June 9, 2000

BIRTHPLACE:
New Brunswick, New Jersey

TURNED PROFESSIONAL:
2016

OLYMPIC MEDALS WON:
1 gold, 1 silver

CHAMPIONSHIPS:
P&G Championships,
Secret US Classic, Pacific Rim
Championships

FAMILY TIES

Laurie was born in New Brunswick, New Jersey, on June 9, 2000. Her full name is Lauren Hernandez.

Laurie's parents are Anthony and Wanda. She has an older brother named Marcus. And, her older sister is Jelysa. Laurie's grandparents are from Puerto Rico.

Laurie's father works at a courthouse. Her mother works with kids at an elementary school.

WHERE IN THE WORLD?

CANADA

Vermont

New Hampshire

New York

Massachusetts

Rhode Island

Connecticut

Pennsylvania

New Brunswick

New Jersey

Maryland

West Virginia

Delaware

ATLANTIC OCEAN

Virginia

N
W   E
S

EARLY YEARS

Laurie grew up in Old Bridge, New Jersey. At a young age, she tried dance classes. But she did not like them. At age five, Laurie started gymnastics lessons. She was a natural talent!

DID YOU KNOW ?
Laurie gave dancing another chance when she appeared on the popular TV show *Dancing with the Stars*.

With lots of practice, Laurie has turned her natural abilities into success.

Rio2016 🌀

STARTING OUT

Maggie Haney has been Laurie's **coach** since Laurie was five years old. Two years later, Laurie started to train for **competitions**.

When Laurie was nine, she began attending USA Gymnastics camps. There, she learned many new skills from other top coaches.

Coach Maggie knows Laurie very well. Maggie creates special routines that fit Laurie's personality.

Laurie trains with **coach** Maggie six days a week. Her parents drive her to the gym early in the morning. Training makes it hard for Laurie to attend a regular school. So, she is homeschooled.

DID YOU KNOW?
In an all-around competition, gymnasts perform in all events. For women, these are balance beam, floor exercise, uneven bars, and vault.

U.S. OLYMPIC
TRAINING SITE

USA
GYMNASTICS

Laurie also trains with the US Gymnastics team. Once a month, Laurie travels to Texas to meet with US team coach Martha Karolyi.

ELITE GYMNAST

When Laurie was 12, she joined the elite level. That meant she could **compete** against top gymnasts around the world.

In 2012, Laurie was in the all-around competition at the US Classic. She came in twenty-first place. Laurie did not let this get her down. Instead, she trained harder.

DID YOU KNOW
Floor exercises are Laurie's favorite.

Laurie has fun when she competes. She is a great performer who often makes playful faces for the judges and fans.

ALL-AROUND SUPERSTAR

Laurie continued to train with **coach** Maggie. Over time, she became a top gymnast. In 2015, she won the US Junior title.

The 2016 Olympic **trials** were held in San Jose, California. Laurie's skills impressed Team USA coach Martha Karolyi. Laurie earned a spot on the team!

In 2016, Laurie competed in the Pacific Rim Gymnastics Championships. The US team won the gold medal.

THE FINAL FIVE

At 16, Laurie was the youngest gymnastics team member. She joined Simone Biles, Gabby Douglas, Madison Kocian, and Aly Raisman. Together, they traveled to Rio de Janeiro, Brazil.

The team was known as the Final Five. They chose the name to honor **coach** Martha. Theirs was the last team Martha would lead at the Olympics.

Two Final Five members competed in the 2012 Olympics in London, England. Aly (*left*) and Gabby (*second from right*) earned team gold medals in 2012.

Coach Martha taught gymnastics for more than 40 years.

All five US team members **performed** well. But Laurie was the most lively! Her scores helped the team earn a gold **medal** in the team **competition**. The US team won by more than eight points. Laurie was an Olympic **champion**!

The Final Five wore special leotards made just for the Olympics. The leotards are always the national colors and have lots of sparkles.

OLYMPIC PERFORMANCE

Six days later, Laurie **competed** in the individual balance beam event. She looked calm and confident. Her **performance** included advanced tumbling moves, leaps, and spins. Laurie went on to win a silver **medal**.

Laurie is known for leaping high off the balance beam and landing gracefully. The balance beam is 4 feet (125 cm) high, 4 inches (10 cm) wide, and 16 feet (500 cm) long.

Laurie scored a 15.333 on the balance beam.

Laurie spots her landing as she flips through the air. This helps her know where to land.

FAN FAVORITE

Laurie has fans on **social media**. Some call her the human **emoji** because of her many facial expressions.

Laurie famously whispered, "I got this" before her balance beam routine at the Olympics. This inspired others to be confident when faced with a hard task.

Four of the Final Five went to the MTV Video Music Awards.

OUTSIDE THE GYM

Laurie's gymnastics training and events keep her busy. When she's not training, Laurie spends time with her family and friends.

In 2016, the Final Five went to New York City, New York. They met the actors from the musical *Hamilton*.

BUZZ

In August 2016, Laurie became a **professional** gymnast. She plans to **promote** many products. Laurie also hopes to be on the 2020 Olympic gymnastics team in Tokyo, Japan. Fans are excited to see what's next for Laurie Hernandez!

Laurie was on the TV show *Good Morning America*. She came on stage in a giant crystal ball!

GLOSSARY

athlete a person who is trained or skilled in sports.

champion the winner of a championship, which is a game, a match, or a race held to find a first-place winner.

coach someone who teaches or trains a person or a group on a certain subject or skill.

competition (kahm-puh-TIH-shuhn) a contest between two or more persons or groups. To compete is to take part in a competition.

emoji (ee-MOH-gee) small images, symbols, or icons used in text fields in electronic communication such as text messages, e-mail, and social media.

medal an award for success.

perform to do something in front of an audience. A performer is someone who performs.

professional (pruh-FEHSH-nuhl) paid to do a sport or activity.

promote to help something become known.

social media a form of communication on the Internet where people can share information, messages, and videos. It may include blogs and online groups.

trial a test of someone's ability to do something that is used to see if he or she should join a team, perform in a play, etc.

WEBSITES

To learn more about Olympic Biographies, visit **booklinks.abdopublishing.com**. These links are routinely monitored and updated to provide the most current information available.

INDEX

Biles, Simone **18, 19, 20, 21, 25, 27**

Brazil **18**

California **16**

championships **5, 14, 16, 17**

Dancing with the Stars (TV show) **8**

Douglas, Gabby **18, 19, 20, 21, 27**

education **6, 12**

England **19**

family **6, 26**

Good Morning America
(TV show) **27**

Hamilton (musical) **27**

Haney, Maggie **10, 11, 12, 16**

Hernandez, Anthony **6, 12**

Hernandez, Wanda **6, 12**

Hispanic **4**

Japan **28**

Karolyi, Martha **13, 16, 18, 19**

Kocian, Madison **18, 19, 20, 21,
25, 27**

medals **4, 5, 17, 19, 20, 22**

MTV Video Music Awards **25**

New Jersey **5, 6, 8**

New York **27**

Olympic Games **4, 5, 16, 18, 19, 20,
21, 22, 24, 28**

Puerto Rico **6**

Raisman, Aly **18, 19, 20, 21, 25, 27**

Texas **13**

United States **5, 10, 13, 14, 16,
17, 20**